Kazimierz – my fascination

Kazimierz Dolny on the Vistula belongs to Polish myths. As we all know, myths live very long, depending not so much on history and geographical conditions, as on the human need to transgress reality.

When dozens of years ago my husband Jerzy, a Lublinian, brought me, a Varsovian, to an untidy little town, where the air was filled with jabbering of Jewish tradesmen and neighing of peasant nags, I felt disgust rather than admiration. But day after day, an extraordinary fascination was slowly overwhelming my reason.

A few holiday months had passed, when in our cottage amidst trees at the opening of a densely wooded ravine, already enchanted by the dual character of Kazimierz, I wrote the book Two Moons.

The first moon, hardly ever touching the ground, cast light on the life of poor, overworked people, who would prefer to sink into oblivion than pursue unworldly sights. The second, a dazzling one, now and then clouded with silver haze, was a planet of artists, painters and musicians, who in the moonshine saw the dawn of freedom from social and professional affairs and the great light of poetry.

What was my fascination born of?

Of the victory of beauty over ugliness; of the enchantment with peaceful ravines and the whisper of the distant river.

The heroes of my book belong to two different strata: the slaves and the dreamers. Although they are playing on the same stage, their roles are contrived to show two contrasting species of man.

Among the dreamers, painters have always been and still are the dominant group. They say a painter never paints at night what he had been bewitched by at daytime. This, however, is not quite true. Both in the open air and in his studio, a painter paints something which is hard to define: atmosphere. The atmosphere of a place that nature has gifted with charm difficult to be rendered by words or a brush. In fact, he paints his own dream.

The book about two moons shining over the small town of Kazimierz was written decades ago. Since then, street names, house façades, fashions, governments and technologies have changed. But the spell emanating from the legend of the "Peasants' King", Casimir the Great, and his love-affair with a Jewish beauty, Esther, still lingers on at Kazimierz on the Vistula. So does the atmosphere of a myth, of something independent of reality. And in the sky over Kazimierz two moons are still shining.

The town administrators have raised a lot of historic buildings from ruin— both from the Piast times and the Renaissance. The bells of the parish church and the monastery go on calling people for the Angelus, noisy tourists fill the streets, and one can hear the murmur of the littered Grodarz … There is no gap in history, for all these things inspire the artists who crave for something better than reality.

Maria Kuncewiczowa

Maria Kuncewiczowa (1899–1989), a famous Polish writer of psychological novels of manners, for many years resident in England; a lecturer in Polish literature at the University of Chicago.

SPORT I TURYSTYKA
WARSAW

Kazimierz

EDWARD HARTWIG
EWA HARTWIG-FIJAŁKOWSKA
Text Jan Bazyl Lipszyc

Dolny on the Vistula

Kazimierz–the town of my youth

This is the title of the one-man show I presented at the gallery of the Museum of Kazimierz a few years ago. The exhibition consisted of photographs saved from the last war, during which, unfortunately, a large part of my collection was destroyed.

I became enchanted with Kazimierz when I was at secondary school. I often visited it and its fine surroundings coming from my "Goat City" of Lublin. I would come by train, or more often, in a cart. But the most attractive way was to walk to Kazimierz from Puławy. The road led through meadows and fields, orchards with plum and apple trees in bloom. At times we passed over a dike along the Vistula or climbed a hill by the river, enjoying the splendid and unforgettable view of the Vistula bends and the escarpment of Janowiec. The landscape changed throughout the seasons of the year like in a kaleidoscope.

Every artist has a different degree of sensitivity, but Kazimierz has always been a magnet for men of arts. Mostly painters came to work here, but also writers, architects, journalists and folk artists. It was a haven for everyone who had a sense of beauty. Before the war, the artistic bohemia of Kazimierz met at the Barens' restaurant. Under its chestnut trees, blooming in spring, or clad in golden colours in autumn, sat the painters who came here at dusk after their daily open-air session, carrying their fresh, colourful canvases with them, barefooted but wearing Basque berets according to the contemporary fashion. That was the way my painter friends dressed. Zenon Kononowicz, Władysław Filipiak, Professor Władysław Michalak—all came from Lublin and were strongly bound to Kazimierz. I also knew Karol Siciński, who wrote an introduction to one of my photographic albums of Kazimierz, published by the Sztuka publishers in Warsaw.

I have always been emotional about Kazimierz. It was my artistic inspiration. The local folk say God created this fine spot on the earth on Sunday, when he was less tired. Hence its unique atmosphere and charm. I have tried to pass my long-lasting deep devotion to Kazimierz to my family, and to my daughter, Ewa Hartwig-Fijałkowska in particular. An artist photographer like myself, she took photographs for this album together with me.

Our collaboration was not only fruitful, but also very pleasant. We walked together or separately along the Kazimierz trails we knew so well. In different weather and different seasons we tried to collect the most diverse photographic material.

I hope I have managed to hand down my interests to the younger generation. I hope our family relay will continue and my artistic and cognitive experience will not be wasted but developed.

What sort of Kazimierz?

A town from tourist guides, described in text-books on the history of architecture, or painted hundreds of times and photographed by generations of tourists? No, not that sort of town. Edward Hartwig, a senior Polish photographer and his daughter, also an artist photographer, show us quite a different Kazimierz: seen from now the sides, now the back. Even more than the famous historic houses, they like to show us the environment of Kazimierz: woods and orchards, flowers, willows, morning mists and the Vistula at every hour of the day and every season of the year.

It is this, Hartwigs' picture of Kazimierz, full of colours and moods, created with passion, sensitivity and artistic temperament of the authors, that amazes us and provokes reflection. What can explain the phenomenon of this small town which for decades has been well known as a pearl of Polish Renaissance? Is it the historical importance of the twin houses of the Przybyła brothers, called St Nicholas' and St Christopher's, of Celej and Górski families, or the White house, or of the parish church and the castle ruins?

Kazimierz would retain its identity even if these Renaissance houses, renovated with so much care, disappeared overnight, for they are not the only sources of its fame. It is revealed by the pictures in this book. Naturally, they include some photographs of the most popular historic monuments of Kazimierz. But the true love of E. Hartwig and his daughter is the town's landscape: shingle roofs, the Vistula at sunset, hills on fire in autumn colours, and dark loess ravines. Maybe the real Kazimierz is that of whitewashed cottages with shingle roofs and wooden arcades and not just the richly decorated houses of the Przybyła brothers, built to demonstrate their owners' wealth.

Everyone can find something different in this album—a Kazimierz of his or her own. Come with us for a walk round the town, its close surroundings and its farther neighbourhood, and through its eight hundred years' history, starting from the times when Kazimierz Dolny on the Vistula did not yet exist.

Kazimierz lies on the Vistula fourteen kilometres from Puławy, on the road to Opole Lubelskie. The town is shaped somewhat like the letter T, with the top part adjoining the Vistula bank and the perpendicular stem stretching along the valley of the small river Grodarz. Squeezed in this valley, the town is overtopped by high loess hills. The one with the donjon is nearly 70 metres high, the one with the castle is 30 metres lower. The town itself is very small. The distance from the chapel in Lubelska Street to the Vistula is no more than a kilometre, and from the Kobiałki granary—the farthest up the river—to the granaries of Mikołaj Przybyła and Feuerstein—2.5 kilometres. Practically all historic buildings of Kazimierz except the granaries can be viewed from the Krzyżowa Góra or from the foot of the donjon. This is what adds charm to the place: it being so compact, so packed within a small area.

Much has been said and written in a scholarly tone about the Mannerist lay-out of the town. In fact, this lay-out has been neither thought out nor designed. The town has developed over centuries. Even the famous axis: the donjon—the castle—the parish church—the Reformed Church and Monastery has resulted from the configuration of the land rather than from any town planning project in the past. It makes the final outcome even more interesting, as it was worked out by generations of industrious burghers and thrifty *starostas*.

The Great or the Just?*

The Kazimierz plateau, a part of the Lublin uplands, had been a good place for settlement from time immemorial. Rich loess soil covering limestone rocks cut with deep ravines encouraged farming and breeding as early as the Neolithic Age, traces of which have been discovered in the vicinity of the town. The Vistula makes its way here between two escarpments. The higher right bank, where the stream Grodarz joins the Vistula, was simply an ideal place to build a fortress in order to defend the river ford. Scholars do not agree on which of the hills the original settlement was built. Maybe it was the Krzyżowa Góra, maybe where now the donjon stands, or the hill with the ruins of the castle. It might have been the present site of the Reformed Church on Plebańska Hill, identified with the historic Wietrzna Góra (Windy Hill). Its other name was Skowieszyn, and Skowieszyn was situated at the source of the Grodarz, where today lies the village of Skowieszynek.

All this took place under Casimir the Just. According to some records, the settlement belonged to the prince until the years 1173–1177. Those were times of unrest. The Vistula valley, which divided the domains of the Piasts and the Ruthenian Ruriks, was continually invaded by Tartars, Lithuanians, Ruthenians and Sudovians. Thus the fortress of Skowieszyn would defend this easy access into the country.

Here Casimir settled Premonstratensian Nuns from the Cracow Zwierzyniec district. Apart from Skowieszyn itself, the convent was endowed with a few villages in the neighbourhood, and on the other side of the Vistula. It was they who called the place Kazimierz, after their benefactor, the ruling prince. Until the 14th century two names were used: the old one, Skowieszyn in official documents, and Kazimierz in everyday language. The settlement, situated at a river ford on the important trade route from Pomerania to Ruthenia, developed despite being threatened by devastating raids, mostly by Tartars, who ravaged the Lublin region nearly every decade. It might have been the reason why this important strategic and mercantile settlement was returned to the royal administration. Anyway, before 1326 it was again the property of the ruler.

The royal estate included the town itself and at least four villages. The Kazimierz castle and its surroundings were bestowed on Cas-

---

* Casimir the Great (1310–1370), King of Poland from 1333, took great care about the development of the country's economic and defensive system. He was called "the great builder" (he erected 50 castles). He signed a treaty with the Teutonic Knights at Kalisz, incorporated the Halicz-Włodzimierz Ruthenia to Poland and subdued Mazovia and Podolia provinces.

Casimir the Just (1138–1194), the youngest of Bolesław the Wry-mouthed's four sons, among whom the king divided the country on his deathbed. Ruled in Poland as senior prince from 1177.

tellan Wilczek of Sandomierz by King Casimir the Great.

It should be explained that there were two castles at Kazimierz. Before the builder-king ordered his castle to be built, there had already stood a donjon on a 78-metre-high nearby hill. It might have been built by Prince Konrad of Mazovia as early as the 1240s, or by King Władysław the Short. The only brick element of the original wooden castle, it is definitely older than the castle of Casimir, built below on the south slope of the hill in the mid-14th century.

Kazimierz became a town under the king whose name it was bearing, Casimir the Great, though this fact is not quite certain. Undoubtedly, it was the third town in the Lublin region, preceded by Lublin and Wąwolnica. Since Kazimierz lay on an important trade route and charged a toll, it developed rapidly. Under King Sigismund Augustus it obtained the right to have three fairs held every year.

The burghers of Kazimierz were shoemakers, fishermen or butchers; they brewed beer and traded in salt. From the 15th century they floated more and more timber down the river and traded in grain, which soon made the town very prosperous. At that time the first granaries were erected. Initially they were built of wood, then wood was replaced by stone which was in large supply, for the whole region sat on limestone.

Before the fast growth of the town and its equally rapid fall are described, it is worthwhile to find the origin of its name, Kazimierz Dolny on the Vistula. For centuries legend has associated the foundation of the town with Casimir the Great. In nearby Bochotnica there still stand the ruins of Esther's castle, where King Casimir the Great was supposedly meeting his Jewish mistress Esther. In fact, she never lived there. As we already know, the town was named after Casimir the Just, although there had already been a settlement there, for the Premonstratensian Nuns were not settled in a vacuum. And what about Casimir the Great? His merits included the granting of a town charter to Kazimierz and the construction of the second castle. But why "Dolny" (Lower)? To avoid confusion, as there was another Kazimierz far on the upper Vistula, today a district of Cracow, then a separate town.

After the fire in 1561 …

… there began a period of the town's prosperity, which lasted until the Swedish invasion. After the fire, which destroyed nearly the whole town, including the parish church, Kazimierz was rebuilt to start its career as a trade centre on the Vistula. From the mid-16th century the exports of grain to Gdańsk by Kazimierz merchants grew quickly. Towards the end of the 16th century Kazimierz became the fifth important grain centre on the Vistula. Grain was imported from distant Russian lands, or bought in the neighbourhood. The town grew rich, its burghers built fine houses and huge granaries. The parish church was reconstructed, the hospital and the Church of St Anne were built. At that time Kazimierz was the second important town in the province. Italians, Scots and people from all over Poland settled here. A good example was the Przybyła family, who belonged to the most powerful grain merchants. From the close of the 15th century Jews began to settle at Kazimierz, and their numbers kept growing steadily until the Second World War.

On 18 February 1656 Charles X Gustav of Sweden crossed the Vistula at Kazimierz and defeated hetman Czarniecki at Gołąb. The Swedes set fire to Kazimierz, whose destruction was compounded the following year by another fire, also due to them. It destroyed the houses between the parish church and Lubelska Street, as well as the castle. As it usually happens in wartime, the fire was accompanied by a plague, which completed the disaster. Besides, the town was regularly plundered by Swedes, Cossacks, Hungarians under Rakoczy and the Polish Commonwealth army. A contemporary royal survey showed that only 37 houses were inhabited and of these seven by Jews. The Swedish invasions resulted in the decline of the great merchant families. Grain trade was continued by the nobility and magnates. This caused the decline of burghers' patronage over the arts and of burghers' culture itself.

The time of devastations over, the town was gradually rebuilt. Its houses and granaries were restored to their former splendour. During the great prosperity era there were about 60 granaries at Kazimierz, half of them of wood. They stood around the port and along the Vistula bank both up and down the river. In 1671 the construction of St Anne's Church on the site of the former Church of the Holy Spirit was completed. About the same time the monastery complex on Plebańska Hill was finally built. The monastery of the Reformed Order was enlarged step by step throughout the whole 17th century.

More defeats and the decline of the town

The period of prosperity was soon over. The 18th century brought new disasters, this time connected with the Saxon wars. Such monarchs as Augustus the Strong, Charles XII and Peter the Great paid visits to Kazimierz. Alas, they brought too many people with them. The result were robberies, fires and poverty. To make things worse, the centuries' long ally—the river—also betrayed the town. This source of the town's well-being, at first providing a ford and then a natural trade route for transporting timber and grain, the Vistula shifted its bed away from Kazimierz in the mid-18th century, thus causing the final decline of granaries. The townsfolk took to timber floating and lime burning, but this did not make things better.

Complete deterioration was brought about by the partitions of Poland. The town came under the rule of the Austrian emperor and was separated by frontiers from Gdańsk and Warsaw, both towns then becoming a food market. The castle was in a state of complete ruin. The 1774 survey found no premises fit for habitation there.

Princess Anna Sapieha purchased Kazimierz in 1819 and Prince Adam Czartoryski of Puławy—ten years later, but it did not help the town. Apart from raising some interest in Kazimierz landscape and architecture, the visits of guests from Puławy changed nothing in the life of the town inhabitants. Anyway, the Czartoryskis owned Kazimierz only for three years. In 1831 Prince Adam had his whole property confiscated for his participation in the national insurrection.

During the insurrection, the division of General Sierawski crossed the Vistula at Kazimierz, while near Karczmiska Lieutenant Colonel Count Juliusz Małachowski was killed defending the ford against the approaching Russians. Two stone slabs commemorate his deed. One of them has been placed at the entry to the ravine bearing his name.

Between the two national insurrections, the burghers at Kazimierz earned their living mainly from tanning. The most renowned tanners were the Ulanowski family. After 1860 grain trade picked up again, but it disappeared for good when a railway was built along the Vistula. In the late 19th century one of the granaries served for nail manufacture and another one as a brewery and then a fruit preserving factory. Some fell into ruin, but most were pulled down. At the end of the century Kazimierz had only 316 houses and 2500 inhabitants, i.e. the same number as in 1627, so the town was obviously in a state of decline. In 1866 Kazimierz was ravaged by another fire, destroying a dozen-odd houses in the marketplace. Three years later the town lost its municipal rights. For many years only its coat of arms, depicting a tower on a crescent, a symbol of guards at the ford, recalled the good times of Kazimierz. It was not until 1927 that the municipal rights were restored to Kazimierz.

No disaster would spare the town. In 1915 its whole north-west area and a part of the marketplace were destroyed by a bombardment. Moreover, after the war, the authorities of the revived Polish state would not permit the renovation of individual buildings still in a passably good state of repair. They were to wait for a general architectural design, which was never drawn up. It was not until Jerzy Siennicki became conservator of the historical relics in Lublin province, that the Górski house was renovated according to his design and under his supervision, although it differed from what the existing documentation showed. The Celej and St Christopher's houses were reconstructed by the architect Jan Witkiewicz-Koszczyc.

The period between the wars was marked by the reconstruction of some historic buildings and by the new trend to build houses for people from the world of culture, who began to settle here. The architect Karol Siciński designed the house of Maria Kuncewicz and her husband Jerzy. The authoress lived there until her death.

The Second World War was as cruel to Kazimierz as the previous ones. The Nazis, whose Gestapo had their headquarters at the monastery of the Reformed Order, exterminated the Jewish population and destroyed the town. They pulled down the north-west and south-west sides of the marketplace. Although Kazimierz was liberated on 28 July 1944, it lay for another half a year on the frontline, which stopped on the Vistula.

After the war, Kazimierz was reconstructed according to the design by Karol Siciński. It was simple and showed a great respect for historical monuments. Since 1947 Karol Siciński was an inventory maker, designer, town-planner and investor at Kazimierz for 11 years. A great part of what we can admire today is his achievement. He was the author of the project to turn the township into a tourist resort. He reconstructed the Marketplace and the finest granaries, and designed many new residential houses. Many of his concepts may be criticized today, but the tastes differed forty years ago. Kazimierz owes the common use of shingle for roofing to Siciński, whose concept of combining the local stone with wood and covering houses with natural materials is generally adhered to nowadays. It has proved most suitable to the character of the town and it creates its unique, enchanting atmosphere, so attractive for tourist these days.

Kazimierz – a painters' town

When writing about Kazimierz, one cannot forget the role of painters in its history. The town has been portrayed by such splendid artists as Zygmunt Vogel, Wojciech Gerson, Michał Andriolli, Józef Brandt, Stanisław Masłowski, Władysław Podkowiński, Leon Wyczółkowski, Władysław Ślewiński, Józef Pankiewicz, Władysław Skoczylas, Piotr Potworowski and Tadeusz Pruszkowski. The latter, rector of the Academy of Fine Arts in Warsaw, initiated student open-air painting at Kazimierz, which made it a painters' town for years. Others deserving mention are painters of St Luke's Fraternity to which belonged Jan Zamoyski, Antoni Michalak, Jan Gotard and Bolesław Cybis; the outsider Feliks Topolski; and the painters working after the Second World War: Zenon Kononowicz, Jan Karmański, Władysław Filipiak. The painters' milieu at Kazimierz had a great impact on the urban growth and cultural development of the town.

Not only painters

These days Kazimierz is crowded with tourists who come to see its famous monuments of the past and its landscape. It is also famed for its open-air painting and admired by writers, journalists and architects. Maria Kuncewiczowa described her place in and way to Kazimierz in her pre-war collection of short stories entitled *Dwa księżyce* (Twoo Moons). Nothing can be added to what she wrote. The painting circles of pre-war Kazimierz were described by Hanna Mortkowicz-Olczakowa in her novel. Kazimierz was also frequented by writers when the war ended. The poet Władysław Broniewski happened to take a bath in the Vistula in full dress, which was said to be connected with his special liking to banqueting on board a ship. Other visitors to Kazimierz were Adolf Rudnicki, Konrad Bielski and Józef Czechowicz.

Kazimierz has also been a favourite subject of photographers, and a number of albums appeared including the earliest one by Jerzy Dzierzbicki, with the preface by Tadeusz Pruszkowski, published in 1933.

Mention is due to the present director of the museum and the town's art conservator Jerzy Żurawski. He looks after the conservation of historical monuments and has renovated many of them. He brought here the 18th-century manor house from Gościeradów, where he now has his office, and a wooden house from the beginning of this century from the town of Puławy.

A wooden presbytery from Karczmiska has also been moved to Kazimierz. All these buildings fit in very well with the old architecture of the town and its atmosphere and they do not spoil its harmony.

Castles, churches, houses, granaries

It would be impossible to describe the atmosphere of an autumn afternoon at the foot of the castle ruins or a spring morning on the Vistula. It has been conveyed by the authors of the album in their pictures. What needs to be described only is what cannot be shown by photographs. And this is history.

Let us start the description of the town and its surroundings from the oldest monument—the donjon. It is a stone structure, now just under twenty metres high. It used to be a little higher when it had battlements. It is ten metres in diameter and the walls are 4.2 metres thick at ground level. There is only one entrance at the height of six metres. Originally, the tower was to defend the crossing of the Vistula and collect customs duties. Later, the defence role was taken over by the castle. As legend has it, the tower served as a lighthouse showing the way to barges on the Vistula with a fire burning on its top. There is a story that the voivode of Poznań Maćko Borkowic, sentenced to prison by Casimir the Great for his robberies and anti-royal activity, starved to death in the vaults of this five-storeyed tower. The castle on the south slope of the hill, definitely built by order of Casimir the Great, is a typical structure of that time. Like the donjon, it was built of the local limestone upon the firm rock. It had a tower facing the Vistula river, a square courtyard, twelve rooms and an entrance gate facing the donjon. A dry moat was later dug in the limestone in front of the gate.

During the Renaissance, the castle was rebuilt by order of *starosta* Mikołaj Firlej in the first half of the 16th century. A brick tower was added, the residential quarters were enlarged. The architect, Piotr Likiel, who supervised the works, gave the structure an ornamental character. It no more played a defensive role, since the techniques of warfare (the use of cannons) required quite different structures. The castle at Kazimierz thus became a residence, but not for long. Destroyed by the Swedish invaders and during Augustus the Strong's armed conflict with Stanisław Leszczyński, it never regained its former splendour. During the Confederation of Bar in 1768 it gave shelter to the confederates who fought against the Russian army. After the bombardment only the framework was left and in 1806 the parapet walls had to be pulled down, as they became dangerously unstable.

Today, like most of King Casimir's castles in

Poland, it is a ruin with some rooms reconstructed to house a museum.

On a hill three kilometres to the north-east stand the ruins of the castle at Bochotnica, in a much poorer state. As you already know, there are no historical records about any stay of Casimir the Great and Esther in the castle, but a legend tells the beautiful story of their love. Let us then believe the legend which calls it Esther's castle.

There is one more castle, situated on the other side of the Vistula. It can be reached via a ford up the Vistula near the quarry.

A Ruthenian voivode, Piotr Firlej, obtained a town charter for the village of Serokomla and named it Janowiec in 1537. In the same year he completed the construction of an imposing residence on a nearby hill. The enormous castle, built on a rectangular plan, with towers in the corners, contained seven halls and 98 rooms. It was inherited from the Firlejs by the Tarło family and later by the Lubomirskis. Plundered and burnt down by the Swedes, it was restored to an even more splendid edifice by Marcin Lubomirski, the extravagant Grand Marshal of the Crown. When it was sold to *starosta* Mikołaj Junosza Piasecki in 1870, the castle began to deteriorate. With its owners changing continually, it fell into complete ruin. The last private owner sold the castle to the Museum of Kazimierz Dolny (now the Vistula Museum) in 1975. Today, the ruin is under conservation and its interiors house a branch of the Kazimierz Museum.

There are three churches at Kazimierz. The oldest of them, the parish church, consists of a nave, a chancel, three chapels and a belfry. The parish church, modernized throughout centuries, is a fine, very impressive structure. The first brick church was built here under Casimir the Great. Though it was mentioned by the chronicler Jan Długosz, it is not known which fragments of the present church have been preserved from that structure. It was burnt in 1561 and in 1580 its reconstruction was started. By 1591 the nave was rebuilt in the Gothic style and then the work was stopped. It was resumed in 1610–1613 in Renaissance style, when the nave walls were heightened, gables changed and a chancel added. An Italian, Jacopo Balin, constructed a barrel vault with lunettes. He built the chancel and gave a Gothic-Renaissance-Mannerist character to the whole structure. Only the west portal and the ogival passage under the belfry remained Gothic. In 1612, Elżbieta Borkowska, daughter of the poet Jan Kochanowski of Czarnolas, founded a chapel on the north side of the church. Even more resplendent is the Górski chapel on the opposite side, founded by the burghers from Góry district in 1625. Six years later it was consecrated. Before 1653, the Radzik couple founded the third chapel, called Różańcowa or Królewska. Nowadays the parish church looks almost the same as three hundred years ago.

The invaluable Przybyła family, whose member Mikołaj launched the reconstruction of the parish church after the biggest fire in the town's history, together with other burghers and the parish-priest Bech, founded the second church at Kazimierz—the Church of the Annunciation to the Holy Virgin Mary. Mikołaj Przybyła donated a plot for the church on Plebańska, or Windy Hill in 1591. On the initiative of Henryk Firlej, the Reformed Order was brought to Kazimierz in 1626 and the small brick church was given to them. The industrious monks immediately started to enlarge the church and twelve years later they began to build a monastery. It was finished in 1690 and the wall around the monastery was erected in the first half of the 18th century.

The town was extremely prosperous in the first half of the 16th century. A hospital, or rather a home for old people, was built of brick. This interesting one-storey house with a much decorated gable looks rather awkward now that Lubelska Street has been elevated by nearly two metres. In 1670, i.e. thirty five years after the construction of the hospital, the adjacent church was completed. Built on the site of a small wooden church, it is a smaller and more modest replica of the parish church. It has no chapels, but the decoration is modelled on that building.

It is time to have a look at the Marketplace and the 15th-century town hall, called the Gałuszewski house, a slightly remodelled building at the corner of Lubelska Street and the Marketplace. Scientific research, Vogel's water-colours from 1792, and 19th-century lithographs and drawings, as well as the houses still preserved give an idea of what the Marketplace looked like in the late Middle Ages and more modern times. Also in the Marketplace stand the twin houses of the Przybyła brothers, St Nicholas' and St Christopher's, known from thousands of photographs and paintings.

Both houses, built in 1615 for the sons of Bartosz Przybyła, have been preserved. They display a variety of sculptural ornamentation – from the portraits of their owners' patron saints to decorative parapets. The decorations include animal and human figures, floral patterns and Latin inscriptions, ancient mythology and Christian symbols. A number of papers have been written about the meaning of these ornaments. It is supposed that their author might have been the parish-priest Wojciech of Żnin. These houses, the richest in the town, demonstrated the importance of the Przybyła family, who owned their riches from trade in grain. The rest of the houses in the Marketplace are much more modest. Some of them have wooden arcades. With their simple form and beauty they are charming and perhaps even finer than the houses of the nouveaux riches – the Przybyłas.

The oldest Renaissance house at Kazimierz stands outside the Marketplace in Senatorska Street. The name of the street comes from later times, when the merchant peak of Kazimierz was already over and the grain trade, some houses and most of the granaries were taken over by the magnates. The house, called Górski, was built in 1607. Destroyed along with other houses in this street by the fire of 1915, it was reconstructed in the 1920s. Unfortunately, the present parapet differs from the original one.

The Celej house, also called Black or St Bartholomew's, is even grander. It boasts the most opulent parapet in Poland. Built by Bartosz Celej, probably an Italian, ca 1630, it was purchased 102 years later from his heirs by the Ulanowskis and then by the Polish government in 1920. Like all historic buildings at Kazimierz, it was several times destroyed and reconstructed. Today the splendid parapet again adorns the façade of the house, now a museum.

The richness of the façades of the Przybyła and Celej houses not only showed the wealth and importance of Kazimierz merchants, but also manifested their Counter-Reformation views and loyalty to the Roman-Catholic church. Such a demonstration of religious beliefs in art was characteristic of Polish Mannerism. At Kazimierz it was stronger than anywhere else.

The third house in Senatorska Street, called Biała (White), stands nearest to the Vistula. The youngest of the houses, it was an imitation of the Celej house, though its parapet is only a faint reflection of the former's one. But its simple, modest and harmonious façade is pleasant to the eye.

The granaries are perhaps the most interesting historical relics of Kazimierz. They are quite unlike any other buildings in our country, architecturally uniform, though differing in ornamentation. The most imposing of them were modelled on Kazimierz churches, especially the parish church. They, too, were supposed to show the wealth of the merchants.

In the years 1568–1597 there were 45 granaries at Kazimierz, of which 39 belonged to the town inhabitants. The granaries were erected in several rows close to the harbour and in one row in the Bochotnica and Cracow suburbs about the same time as the houses at Kazimierz, i. e. the early 17th century. These solid structures of local stone, with thick walls, had two or three storeys and were divided into two symmetrical halves. Many of them had high annexes in front which served as loggias. The finest granary, called Pod Bożą Męką (The Wayside Shrine), built by Wawrzyniec Górski in 1625, is known only from drawings. The price of the Przybyłas' granary called Pod Jeleniem (The Deer) in 1657 gives an idea of their value. It was worth 3,000 Polish zlotys, that is 500 zlotys more than St Christopher's house. Only ten granaries have survived to our time, four of them in ruin, including the Przybyłas' granary, now a natural science museum, the Feuerstein's in Puławska Street, a half of the Bliźniaczy (Twin) granary and the Kobiałki granary at the other end of the town up the Vistula, now housing a tourist hostel. Also the outside walls of the granary in Puławska Street near the town centre have survived. Even these scarce remains show that they were modelled on the Renaissance parish church. It is quite evident in their ornamentation, especially that of the façades.

Upon the hills and on the Vistula

The historical relics of Kazimierz could be described in a greater detail, for to many of them numerous scientific studies and extensive literature have been devoted. But it is more exciting to follow the photographers to small alleys behind the Marketplace, to look at the back of the parapet crestings, to stare at the synagogue turned into a cinema, or to reflect for a while at the monument to the memory of Jews murdered at Kazimierz. The monument, designed by the architect Tadeusz Augustynek in 1978, stands at Czerniawy, by the highway. Founded by the Vistula museum, it was built of tombstones from the Jewish cemetery destroyed by the Germans. One should also climb the Hill of Three Crosses called Krzyżowa Góra as early as before 1577 and nobody knows why. It offers a matchless view of Kazimierz. Then there are lovely walks along ravines cut out of rich loess, particularly in May, with flowers all around, or in late September, when the hills over Kazimierz shimmer with gold, red, and every shade of brown colour.

We suggest a walk up the river, passing by the Kobiałki granary, to the Janowiec ford and the quarry, and further to the windmill, brought there from Mięćmierz, and visible from a long distance. Or in the opposite direction–to Esther's castle above the neighbouring village of Bochotnica, and then over the hills as far as the avenue of giant old poplars in the suburbs of Puławy.

To get acquainted with Kazimierz you need plenty of time. The town must be learned at a slow pace, viewed from different sides, at various times of day and all seasons of the year, from the Vistula to the hills rising above. You must look from the donjon to the Reformed Church and from the Reformed Church to the parish church, the castle and the donjon. You should see the panorama of hills on the other side of the Vistula and cross it to the Janowiec castle. You ought to come and see the festival of folk bands and drop in on a still winter day to see an empty Marketplace and buy a cake in the shape of a cock without queueing for it. Only then can you say that you know Kazimierz, that you have really seen it.

◄ 1. In the autumn

2. The old river bed

3. When all around is in bloom ...

4. Where there is limestone, there are caves—an entrance to one

5. ... and its inside

6. Limestone hills, white like Carrara marble
7. Destroyed and burnt down by Swedes, Russians and Germans, the town has never been overcome by the several wars throughout six centuries
8. Ruins of Esther's castle; in fact she never even visited it

9. Autumn ploughing ▶

10. High water is coming
11. Paradise for ducks

12. Feuerstein's granary; in its hey-day the town had fifty or so such granaries by the Vistula
13. The castle seen from below the tower

14. As some people claim, an underground tunnel cut in the limestone once connected the castle with the tower
15. All is golden and red

16. Ravines cut in the soft loess   17. Autumn over the hills

18. The Mannerist axis of the town–from the Reformed Church to the tower

19. The parish church has overtopped the Kazimierz marketplace for more than 400 years now

20. View from the Hill of Three Crosses over the
Reformed Church

21. Casimir at Kazimierz

22. This is a picture that has not been painted by artists
23. Folk dancers from the Kurpie region in the Old Marketplace
24. Folk art is full of colours

25. Fire-brigade at drill looks quite spectacular
26. How many pictures are painted every year
in the town?
27. These houses are not so rich as those of the
Przybyła brothers, but without them the town
would not be what it is

28. At the foot of the castle
29. Lubelska Street joining the Marketplace
30. Stones and wooden shingles – that is the style
of the town

31. The most opulent parapet in Poland
—on the Celej house

32. Museum of goldsmith craft
33. Kazimierz still subsists on painters ...
and their means of subsistence
depend on the town

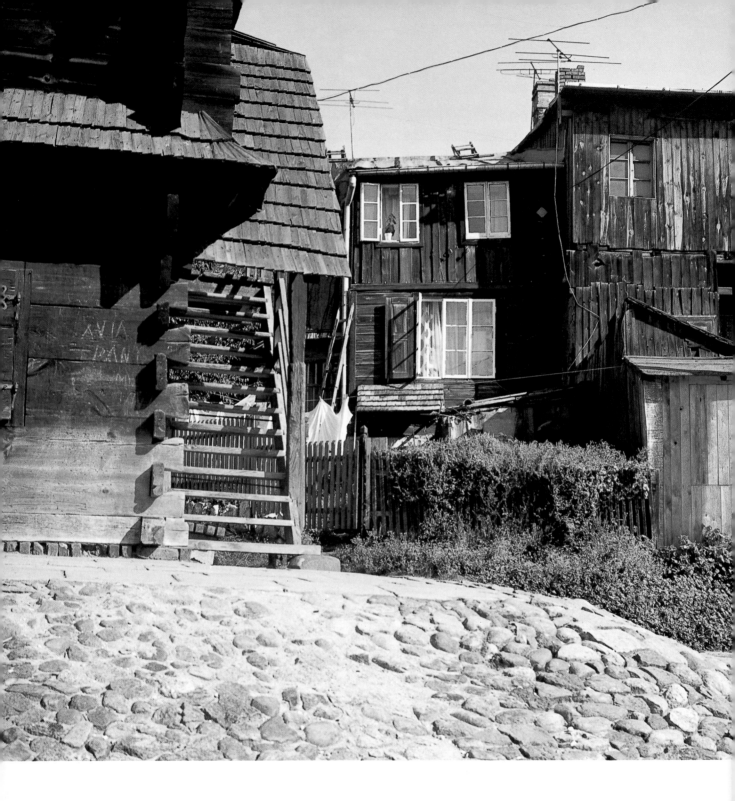

34. Not only Renaissance houses 35. At the back of the Marketplace

36. What peace, what quietness …

37. Like in a fairy-tale …

38. Once the biggest river port of the Polish Commonwealth existed here

39. In this house, designed by Karol Siciński, lived the famous writer, Maria Kuncewiczowa

40. … this is what orchards overgrowing the hills look like

◄ 41. Colours, colours …
42. Marsh marigolds and apple trees are marks
of spring at Kazimierz

43. Limestone for granaries and houses
is not extracted here
44. The Vistula banks near Kazimierz
are mostly high escarpments

◀ 45. A romantic sunset and a down-to-earth dredger   46. Potato lifting

47. Blackthorns and marsh marigolds in bloom

48. Autumn colours and the white loess escarpments

49. Quite recently the Vistula bank has been
decorated with a windmill from Męćmierz

50. The orchard and the bees are the same
as in old times, but the bee-hives differ

51. It is most lovely in late September

52. A heavy ear bending down to the ground ▶

53. It is already the height of summer

54. Autumn once again

55. There is a lot to be protected in the
Kazimierz Landscape Park

56. View of the Krzyżowa Góra from Kazimierz

57. The river embraced by its high banks

58. Pines, birches, oaks, beeches ... ▶

59. Willows … and flowers
60. The Vistula spreads wide, but it is not always
so shallow and placid

61. The Vistula sands ▶

◄ 1. An avenue of poplars leads out of Puławy towards Kazimierz

2. Kazimierz is a town of painters, who paint not only in the Marketplace

3. Hops grow well here, too

4. Just—willows

5. Road to Parchatka

6. Somewhere on the Vistula

7. Untouched by modern civilization ▶
8. Swampy meadows by the river

9. On the meadows …

10. ... in peace

13. Picture of Kazimierz – in an
old granary

14. Mikołaj Przybyła's granary – now
a natural science museum

15. As most granaries, this one was modelled on the
Renaissance gables of the parish church

16. Only some walls have remained of this granary

17. The organ in the parish church, the most important of Kazimierz churches; the wood-carving in the Gdańsk style shows the mastery of early 17th-century craftsmen

18. West side of the parish church with the remodelled Gothic belfry over the entrance

19. Oak door with rich Baroque ornamentation set
into a Gothic portal
20. View from the parish church over the Marketplace
and the Gdański house

21. Entrance to the parish church under the tower ▶
22. Beneath the parish church

23. The tower measures some twenty metres in height and more than thirty in circumference
24. The parish church, the castle and the tower all seem to be one monument of history

25. The castle seen ▶ from the parish church
26. These crosses commemorate an 18th-century plague, but the name Krzyżowa Góra is a few centuries older

27. This view has been painted so many times before
28, 29. Festival of Folk Bands and Singers

30. View from the Marketplace
over St Anne's Church

31. Evening at Kazimierz

32. Shingle roofs are enchanting

33. It is a pity that the front wall of the hospital
is hidden behind a street (at the background
the hospital church of St Anne)

34. Kazimierz roofs

35. Kazimierz is asleep, waiting for the spring to come

36. Luckily, it was not covered with asphalt

37. How many fairs have already been held in this marketplace?

38. Since the reign of King Sigismund I and his son Sigismund Augustus Kazimierz has been entitled to have three fairs a year

39. Open-air painting ▶ like in the time of Professor Pruszkowski
40. Palette of an artist from Kazimierz

41. By a well, when chestnut trees are in bloom   42. A different look of the well in the Marketplace

43. View of the Reformed Church
from the Marketplace

44. Tomasz Drzazga's Gallery
45. A bit more modern Kazimierz than in the Marketplace

46. In the Old Marketplace
47. Once the town supplied quite distant regions ▶ with wicker hoops

48. Old baths

49. Tiny steets, parish church, tower …

50. The houses
of the Przybyłas
— St Nicholas'
and St Christopher's

51. St Christopher
52. Mythology and
saints, rich
ornaments and
Latin inscriptions

53. Fragment of the parapet wall on one of the
Przybyła houses

54. Przybyła houses seen from below the arcades
of the neighbouring house

55. The parapet of the Celej house
56. Celej house—all its beauty displayed

57. There is no other parapet so rich as the ▶
one on the Celej house
58. Its rear looks even more unique

59. By the wall of the Reformed Church

60. Monastery on the Plebańska, or Windy Hill

61. This well stands in the monastery courtyard

62. This is how water was drawn for long centuries

63. Chapel under the wall of the
Reformed Church ...
64. Students paint everywhere and everything

65. It is not easy to live here in winter …   66. Coming back from the market

67. Ravines
68. This relief on the riverside hills has been made by water and wind

69. Professor Pruszkowski ravine
70. ... it is quiet and lovely also in winter

71. Kobiałki granary—a tourist hostel

72. There are at least six wells like this at Kazimierz
73. Drying hops

74. Wooden Kazimierz

75. Roadside shrine

76. Former quarry, now
re-cultivated

◄ 77, 78. Monument made of the remaining tombstones from the Jewish cemetery, designed by Tadeusz Augustynek in 1978

79. Water, sand and ... sunset

80. Under the castle at Janowiec   81. The walls of the Janowiec castle still stand ...

82. The castle used to dominate
the town

83. A manor house at Moniaki—a start for a regional museum   84. Always to the sun

85. Autumn bonfires
86. Three crosses from the castle at Janowiec – not the
ones on Krzyżowa Góra

87. It looks like covered with silver ▶

Translation
Elżbieta Kowalewska

Graphic design
Tadeusz Kobyłka

Editor
Elżbieta Radziszewska

Technical editor
Mirosława Bombała

ISBN 83-217-2888-X

First Edition
Printed by INTERDRUCK Leipzig GmbH